42 more Heartwarmin' Expressions

A Workbook for Crafting Painting or Stitching

by Sandy Redburn & Shelly Ehbrecht

Crafty Secrets Publications
15430 78A Ave.
Surrey, B.C. Canada
V3S 8R4

ISBN 0-9699410-5-6

Table of Contents

Category Themes

There is a smorgasbord of creative supplies and helpful aids for lettering expressions onto an almost endless array of surfaces. Check with your local retail stores for products from the manufacturers listed below.

Permanent Markers
EK Success
(Zig Markers)
611 Industrial Rd.
Carlstadt, NJ 07072-6507
Phone (201) 939-5404
Fax (201) 939-4511

Permanent Markers
Sakura of America
(Pigma® Ink Products)
30780 San Clemente St.
Hayward, CA 94544-7131
Phone (510) 475-8880
Fax (510) 475-0973

Needle Craft Alphabets
ASN Publishing
1455 Linda Vista Drive
San Marcos, CA 92069
Phone (760) 471-2320
Fax (760) 591-0230

Transfer Paper
Saral Paper Corp.
322 W 57th St.,
Suite 30-T
New York, NY 10019
Phone (212) 247-0460
Fax (212) 247-3046

Introduction

Well, here we are back with a second helping of Heartwarmin' Expressions! We've had so much fun with our first book and such a great response that we decided to warm some hearts again. This book actually began to materialize before we went to press with the first edition. Once we got on a roll we couldn't stop. We hope this brand new collection will leave your imagination and creative spirit brimming with inspiring ideas for using Heartwarmin' Expressions.

Studies in global interests and trends show many of us are looking for more simple pleasures in our complex, often stressful world. We have become more focused on our spirituality, values, family, friendships, homes and health. Adding heartwarmin' and humorous expressions to giftware, greetings, wearables, seasonal and home decor craft projects is an easy and fun way to create more warm fuzzies and smiles in your life and the lives of others.

Your local craft store can present you with a multitude of new creative possibilities. You can also recycle and transform almost any tired old surface into a treasured keepsake or whimsical feel good statement.

Thanks Are Due

We would like to thank the many creative souls who passed on their favorite expressions to be included in this second Heartwarmin' book. A special thanks must go to Raven Regan and to Brenda Rintisch for their great contributions and creative inspirations. We tried to give credit to expressions we could trace an origin to. This proved very difficult as expressions, proverbs and sayings are so widely used and often changed. If you know of names we've missed, or you want to send us some of your own expressions, please drop us a line at Crafty Secrets Publications. A big thank you to those who do!

Shelly has received her CDD, (Certified Demonstrators Diploma) and enjoys teaching folk art painting and creative lettering classes. She is also a registered nurse on a maternity ward and lives a happy, busylife with her husband and two daughters.

We would also like to thank our husbands and daughters very much, for their loving support and creative feedback. They even got into the brainstorming act with us and came up with some great expressions. They also deserve a big round of applause for doing all the chores and eating all those lousy dinners!

Also, a heartwarmin' thanks to YOU for buying our book!

Sandy & Shelly

Sandy's dedication to inspiring others' creativity includes teaching seminars, writing and publishing books since 1993, including "Crafty Marketing - Jumpstart Your Craft Business". She runs her successful home-based business with the help of her other passion, her husband and three daughters.

Easy Lettering Tips & Tricks

Lettering is not as hard as you may think and, as you will see throughout this book, by no means does it have to be perfect or for that matter straight! You can do your lettering by free hand, or you can trace our expressions and designs right onto your project.

If you would like your lettering larger, you can recreate any expression using the enlarged alphabets in the back of this book. You may also photocopy any expressions and have them enlarged or reduced to fit your personal needs.

It' s Easy!

1. Use a pencil & ruler. Lettering does not have to be even - just consistent.
2. Hold pens in an upright position.
3. When possible pull your pen rather than push.
4. Add extra embellishments to create different styles.
5. Get bravely creative - but remember practice and patience.

Dot lettering seems to be the most popular and easiest style of printing to reproduce. Remember you do not have to embellish your letters with dots. As you will see, you can change your printing style by adding hearts, stars, flowers, snowflakes, holly, stitching lines and more!

There are countless design books available, with wonderful patterns to which you can trace and add expressions. Look around you for inspiration and designs that you can match with expressions. Once you start, you will find life offers endless "perfect spots" to add a Heartwarmin' Expression or tickle some funny bones.

Trace or pencil on your lettering first, to get your spacing right. A good eraser and see-through plastic ruler are two very helpful tools for lettering.

Using Pens & Markers

Using Pens and markers is easy and fun because they are now available in a multitude of tip styles, sizes and colors in both water based and permanent inks. Water based pens work well for a variety of paper crafts, but permanent pigma ink markers won't fade and can be used on a large variety of surfaces. The manufacturers of these markers all agree you should hold your pens in an upright position so the tip has full contact with the writing surface. It may feel a bit awkward but will give you the true essence of the pen tip. You will also find you have better control of your pen when you pull it towards you rather than pushing it away.

Our samples below show how different combinations of pen tips can give your lettering loads of personality and style.

Letters - Pigma Graphic 3,
Stitch lines Pigma Micron 01

Letters - Pigma Graphic 3,
Outline - Pigma Micron 03
Stars - Pigma Micron 01

Letters - Pigma Micron 05
Embellishments - Pigma Micron 01

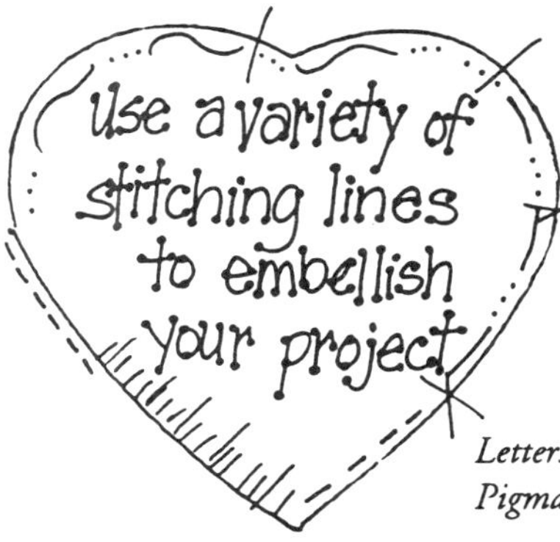

Letters & Borders - Pigma Micron 03

Letters - Zig 08 Millennium, Holly & Berries - Pigma Micron 03, Snowflake & Borders - Pigma Micron 01

Creative Possibilities

Transferring expressions and designs is not difficult. You can mix and match expressions with any pattern and design. Once you decide on an expression and image you want to use, lay tracing paper over it and draw it out. Lay your traced design on your project surface and slip some transfer paper in between your design and prepared surface. Trace the outline with a stylus or empty pen tip. Saral® manufactures a Wax-Free Transfer paper that works on paper, wood, fabric, metal, glass, tile, ceramic, etc. Wax free paper will not clog the tips of your markers and pens. Heat activated transfer pencils also work well on fabric.

Expressions On Wood

There are so many different painting styles, techniques and decorative finishes used on wood today, it can make your head swim. Some popular applications include primitive to fancy overlay stencils, block printing, antiquing, faux finishing, traditional tole painting, pen and ink watercolors, rustic country or folk art painting. You just need to match your design to the right expression and style of lettering. For example, a lovely tole painted floral design would suit a beautifully handwritten expression.

If you don't have a steady hand for doing your lettering with a paintbrush don't worry, you can cheat and use permanent markers. When you apply dots to letters on wood, use paint rather than your pen tip. Not only will you save the life of your pens, you can create dots faster and more consistent in size using paint. Dots can be made using a brush tip, stylus or embossing tool. We use corsage pins and various plastic headed pins for different size dots. Stick the pins into the eraser tip of a pencil and just dip the head into paint. When using permanent markers for lettering, test any varnish first. Krylon manufactures sprays and varnishes that won't make the ink in permanent markers bleed.

Expressions On Paper Crafts

Use expressions to create your own special occasion and seasonal decorations, birthday cards, photo memory albums and scrapbooks, framed calligraphy, greeting cards, gift tags, invitations, stationary and wrapping paper. Jazz up your projects with colored pencils and inks, watercolors, metallic markers, glitter pens, decorative punches and scissors, templates, stencils, stickers, rubber stamps, 3D or traditional decoupage, paper mold reliefs and more!

Painting Expressions On Fabric

First pre-wash fabric to remove any sizing and don't use any fabric softener. You can use a heat activated transfer pencil, or place some fabric transfer paper between your design and fabric (following all manufacturers' directions). Before painting your transferred design, place a piece of card-board under your fabric surface (a cookie sheet will also work). Use fabric paints or regular acrylics mixed with a textile medium. Look for quality brushes recommended for textile painting, fabric markers, or use the mini tips on paint bottles to do your lettering.

Expressions On Glass & Ceramics

Paint expressions on an assortment of dishware, tiles, glasses, vases and decor. You can use traditional ceramic techniques and glazes, or cheat and use the new glass and ceramic paints. DecoArt makes Ultra Gloss, a paint which becomes permanent when baked in your oven. Delta Perm Enamel is a new air drying permanent paint made for glossy and hard to adhere surfaces.

Expressions By Needle & Thread

Stitching includes an array of techniques for applying expressions, using fancy threads, floss, yarns, ribbons or beads. Machine or hand embroidery, hand stitching on felt, needlepoint, cross stitch, plastic canvas, quilted appliqués and silk ribbon embroidery are all popular decorative embellishments. You can stitch expressions on baby bibs to bumper pads, decorative pillows, wall samplers, aprons, linens, sweatshirts, vests, jumpers, jean jackets, boxer shorts, ties, bathrobes and more!

The American School of Needlework (ASN Publishing) has a wonderful book called *365 Cross Stitching Alphabets.* And, if you don't want to stich by hand, check out the amazing things you can create with an embroidery machine today!

Embellishing Your Expressions

Depending on the materials and style of your project you can also embellish expressions with raffia, jute, wire, paper twist, ribbons, lace, trims, buttons, charms, shells, fabric motifs, lace appliqués or miniature accessories. To add unique appeal to cloth dolls and animals use short expressions on mini signs or cut out shapes.

You are only limited by your imagination, so go on . . . get creative!

Angels & Fairies

Angels Welcome Here

Angels lend a helping hand.

Fly with the angels
Dance with the stars

God Can't Be Everywhere
So He Created Angels

Do not fear...
Angels are near

Believe in heavenly things.

I believe in fairies.

Nothing can be truer than fairy wisdom

Tole fairies workshop

Fairy Dust
5¢

Magic happens to those who believe
in fairies

An Angel To Watch Over Me

Grandma's Little Angels
Welcome Here.

The angels danced
the day you were born

Rest Your Wings

Music is the angels talking.

A "cupig" to watch over you.

Angels point the way

Light fades, stars appear
our guardian angel watches here.

Problems are.....
Angels of Opportunity in Disguise.

When in doubt ~ wing it

Bless all creatures great and small.
Noah and Co.

Bless This Home
Oh Lord We Pray
Keep it Safe by Night & Day

The Brightest Love
Shines From Up Above

I love God and God loves me
God bless my family and God bless me

Thanksgiving should be Thanksliving

Dear God and angels up above

Please bless this home With lots of love.

Bless This Home
&
All Who Enter

Bless this home with love and laughter

Count Your Blessings
Instead of Sheep

Be a living expression of God's kindness.
Mother Teresa

God Rest Your Love Upon This Door
&
Bless This Home Forever More

Prayers go up
Blessings come down

Happy Holly Jolly Days

CHRISTMAS

Meowy Chris-mouse.

Yule is Cool.

Snowmen = water retention

There's no business like SNOW business.

Christmas is ....
when you realize how many people
you know and
how many sizes you don't!

HELP WANTED:
See Santa

Santa loves his garden
How does it grow?
With sugar plums & candy canes
row by row
tended by his ho ho hoe

Santa Claws

Santa Paws

We believe in the spirit of Christmas

Tis the season
when silent night is heard everywhere.

Deck the halls.

Christmas Cheer "Reins" here.

CHRISTMAS

Mittens mittens everywhere
But never can we find a pair.

Have a COOL Christmas

WANTED
Jolly men bearing presents

Dear Santa,
We've left some cookies
for you to eat,
so take a wee break
and rest your feet.

Merry
"Kiss"mas

Christmas.....
a very Santa-mental time.

CHRISTMAS.....
A Claus for celebration

We Still Believe

Tis the season of peace & goodwill
until you go shopping

Each snowflake brings to mind
How special you are
You're one of a kind

My Heart Belongs
To Santa

There's no time like snow time

Country

Keep the sunny side up

Never judge a day by the weather.

Good Moos Welcome Here

Cow country  watch your step.

You can "cow"n't on me.

My "udder" house is cleaner.

Udderly Awesome

"Cow"n't your blessings.

Barnyard Friends are Best.

My Heart is Udderly Country

A farmer is a man outstanding in his field.

Never ask a cowboy how wide his spread is

Never squat with yer spurs on.

Please remove your spurs before getting into bed.

Hitch Your Wagon To a Star

-Ralph Waldo Emerson

Blaze your own trail.

Mind your pa and ma.

Live Now

The dust will settle later

Were you raised in a barn?

Ya'll come back now ya hear

MOM is WOW upside down.

♥ Mother ♥
♥ Maker of Miracles ♥

♥ Mom's Mood-o-meter ♥
♥♥ Wonderful ♥♥
♥ Good ♥
• So-So •
Ask Dad.

We laugh, we cry
We make time fly by
Best friends we are
My mom and I!

Motherhood
God's highest calling.

Motherhood is not for wimps.

Mom's stressed. HUGS=RELIEF.

I love to give homemade gifts
which one of the children would you like?

Dad is a banker
provided by
Mother Nature

My Dad is part
He-man
Superman
Tarzan
and Handyman.
He can even scare away
the Boogeyman!

DAD
King of the Remote Control

Dad's Fixin' Shop
Broken Toys & Feelings
Mended For Free

Dad's Corner
NO NAGGIN

FAMILY

Chance made us sisters
But ♥ made us friends.

Sisters are joined
♥ Heart to Heart. ♥

Attention All Teenagers
"NO" is a complete sentence.

Our family's love is tied together
♥ with heartstrings. ♥

Grandpa—
the next best thing to Santa Claus.

Keeper of Family
Folklore & Tales

Grandmas are just moms
with a lot of practice.

You can't scare me
I have grand children.

Grandmas are angels in training.

Shhh... baby's dreaming

Twins are two-two much.

A baby brings a little bit of heaven
down to earth.

Small wonders bring special joys!

♥ When a child is born- an angel sings.

Born to Fish
Forced to Work

Fishing isn't a matter
of life & death.....
It's much more important.

Fish sure grow.....
between the nibble
and the time they get away.

If this hat's missin'
I've gone fishin'

Fishing..... a reel sport.

A reel expert can tackle anything.

Wishin' I was fishin'

A fisherman often comes home with no fish
and a pack of flies.

Early to bed,
Early to rise,
Fish all day
Tell BIG lies.

Fish don't brag
about the size of fishermen
they get away from

Friends like heirlooms
are special treasures

FRIENDSHIP

Whenever
I count my blessings
you're on my list.

Chance made us neighbours but
♡'s made us friends.

Friends are the best collectibles

Like a cup of tea,
friends make you feel
all warm inside.

Friendship warms the ♡
and heals the soul.

Making a friend takes a moment
Being a friend takes a lifetime

Friends like you are precious few.

If friends were roses
I'd pick YOU!

Friendship & Laughter
Are Music For the Soul

Friends Like You Are Far and Few

I don't repeat gossip......so listen closely.

I just ate my willpower.

Madness takes its toll.
Please have exact change.

Dear Lord,
If you can't make me skinny,
make my friends fat.

Lord help me.......
The devil wants me fat!

He who dies with the most toys —
still dies.

Star light star bright
Where the heck is Mr. Right?

I'm in transcendental vegetation.

Everyone's entitled to my opinion.

If they can send one man to the moon
Why can't they send them all?

When opportunity knocks, open the darn door.

Sometimes the best man for the job
is a woman.

If your ship hasn't come in
swim out to it.

Husband and dog missing,
Reward for dog.

Sometimes I wake up GROUCHY
Sometimes I let him sleep.

Funny Bone Ticklers

Behind every good man .....
is a surprised mother in law.

It takes a lot of talent
to get a month behind
in just one day

God put me on this earth to accomplish
a number of tasks.....
I'm so far behind I'll never die.

I'm an Atheist - Thank God.

In God We Trust
all others must pay cash

With my luck I'll be at the airport
when my ship comes in.

I'm not lazy,
I'm motivationally impaired.

Mental floss prevents moral decay.

If at first you do succeed
try not to look surprised

At first I was hesitant
now I'm not sure!

Broken cookies
don't have calories

Hand over the chocolate and
Nobody will get hurt.

Eat, drink and be merry.....
for tomorrow we diet!

Weight has a way
of snacking up on you

If you don't chew your food—
who will?

I can see clearly now...
my brain is gone

Ever stop to think
and forget to start again?

Ewe's not fat
Ewe's woolly fluffy

Ewes Udderly Welcome

furry friends

Ruler of the Roost

Welcome To Our Coop

I woolly wuv ewe.

Friendship is me & ewe!

Remember ....
"Paws" for thought

One Spring Chicken
&
An Old Crow Live Here

Forget the Dog -
Beware of the Owner

This place is for the birds

LOVE builds the warmest nests.

Feathered friends til' the end

When things are RUFF—
Everyone needs a pet

No hen-picking allowed!

I'm having a BAD HARE DAY!

All I Have I Owe To Udders

I love ewe– moo & moo

A spoiled rotten cat lives here.

"Meow" spoken here.

A cat is just a furry little kid.

Cats leave footprints on your heart.

No home is complete without the pitter patter of kitty's feet.

Gardening Angels Plant Seeds of Love

What you sow
is what you grow

♥ Sow kindness ♥
♥ Gather love. ♥

Thyme began in a garden.

Every bunny loves a garden.

Somebunny's been eating the vegtables

Take Thyme
To Smell the Flowers

Sunshine & seeds – scatter every where.

Gardening Angels From Up Above
Please Watch Over This Garden With Love

♥ Meet me at the Garden Gate

Gardening

Keeper of the Garden

One who plants a garden plants happiness

No rain - No rainbows

You make my ♥ bloom

Old gardeners never die
They just spade away.

I'm in therapy and gardening is cheaper than a psychiatrist

Flowers For Thee
With Love From Me

Garden Memories

A garden unearths part of our childhood,
of backyard memories and everything good.
Of marvelous mud pies, rocks and bugs,
mending scrapped knees with Mothers hugs.
But most of us can best recall,
picking a fistful of flowers
with magical powers,
to light up our Mothers face.

Love Faith Wisdom Joy

The Stepping Stones in the Garden of Life

The only thing I grow in my garden is tired

May all your weeds be wild flowers.

Golf is a ball......
no matter how you slice it.

If I can't be seen
I'm on the green

How to get more distance out of your drives:
Hit the ball and run backwards

It takes a lot of balls to golf the way I do.

I'd give up golf if I didn't have so many sweaters
— Bob Hope

Happiness is a hole in one.

Golf or my wife ???
When's tee time?

Ever stop to think...
what GOLF spells backwards
— Al Boliska

Now that I'm older
I can hit the ball out of sight.

No matter if you hook or slice,
your better than par
on the fairway of life

My other car is a broom.

Witch Way?

Fright turn → Witchful Thinking

Hallowe'en Menu
Moanday to Frightday
Ham boogers
Apple spider
Ice Scream
Hallow weiners
Rice creepies
Boo Bury Pie
Fresh Baked Dread
Coffin Drops
Mice Pudding
Foolish goulish
sticky goo cooked
just for you.

Fly our scare plane
Ghost to Ghost
Bone Voyage

The First Wealth is Health

Be the change you want to see in the world
Ghandi

Protect Mother Nature
She's the oldest mom around.

Earth Day is Every Day

If you pray for rain ......
be prepared to deal with some mud.

Brains Are Soft
Helmets Are Hard
Use Both!

He who laughs, lasts.

Laughter is.....
sunshine in the heart
and wings on the soul.

NO Smoking Purdy Please

HUGS - not drugs

Recycle toucans
or 3 cans
or 4 cans.

Keep our rainforests
WET & WILD.

Save our animals
It's a tall order.

Beauty comes in all sizes.

Don't waste water
It's a CATastrophe.

POLLUTION
It's a WHALE of a problem.

All Roads Lead to Crafting

Tole fairies workshop

Knitters like "purls"

If it doesn't move — paint it!

"Craft Show Junkie"

MOM'S WORKSHOP
Enter at Your
Own Risk

Paint til you faint!

The best gifts are always handmade

I only craft on days
that end with Y

CAUTION
Craftaholic in Residence

When the chips are down
Yell BINGO

Was there life
B 4
Bingo

When I grow up
I want to be an actor,
because then I don't have to grow up

You're tu-tu much

Ballet keeps you on your toes

ACTING builds CHARACTER

Bowling is a ball.

If there's no Internet in Heaven
I'm not going

File not found.
Should I fake it?
Yes __ No __

My eyes are square
Cuz I can't quit playing
With my software.

Smash forehead on keyboard to continue

**Proofread carefully
to see if you any words out**

HOMESPUN

HOME

May Our Home Be Warm
And Our Friends Be Many

Home is Where Your Honey is

A happy home is filled ♥ ♥ ♥
♥ With love & laughter. ♥

May Peace Be With You
While You Stay
&
Joy Be With You
On Your Way

A house is built with boards & beams
A home is built with love & dreams.

♥ ♥ ♥ How often thoughts & hearts return....
to the home that's filled with love ♥ ♥ ♥

♥ Home is where the hugs are. ♥

Home is where MOM is!

TRAILER ♥ SWEET ♥ TRAILER

Home for the Harvest

Attention Spiders - Don't worry
We keep house casually.

Home
of a
Domestic
Goddess

$ All work and no pay
makes a housewife $

My idea of housework is to sweep the
room with a glance.

What's a nice girl like me doing in a place like this?

Laundry Room
Drop your pants here.

After ecstacy ......
the laundry.

Motherhood is loads of fun

Housework makes your hare turn gray.

Please Wipe Your Hooves

This isn't clutter...
These are my antiques

If a man's home is his castle...
let him clean it!

Inspiration

The sky is the limit when your ♡ is in it!

Wish it
Dream it
Do it

We can't all be stars but we can all twinkle.

What lies behind us and
What lies ahead of us
Is nothing compared to
What lies within us

Those Who Wish to Sing
Always Find a Song

Improvement begins with I !

Life is like a canvas
Make yours a masterpiece

Happiness is where you find it.

Celebrate LIFE

Think big thoughts
but relish small pleasures

Live Your Live as an Exclamation
Not an Explanation

Happiness is best kept when given away

Beauty is Internal

Don't dream it,
Be it!

We create our tomorrows
by what we dream today.

If it is to Be
It's up to Me

Wine is bottled poetry.

— Robert L. Stevenson

TODAY'S MENU
Two Choices....
Take it or Leave it

Enjoy Life -
I'ts Delicous

Recipe for a happy heart
2 c. love
1 c. friendship
1 c. gratitude
Add a dash of laughter &
Pour into any soul.

Bone Appetit

Real men wear aprons.

Never trust a skinny cook.

You're only cooking up trouble
When you stew about tomorrow.

Only the pure of heart can make good soup

— Ludwig Van Beethoven

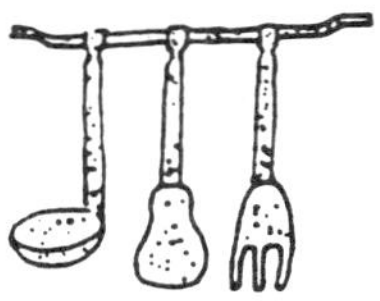

Chocolate is an essential nutrient.

Crumbs of happiness....
makes a loaf of contentment.

This Kitchen is Closed
Due to Illness
I'm sick of cooking

This Kitchen is Seasoned With Love

Friendship
hits the
spot.

Coffee or a pot of tea?
Please sit and share
A cup with me.

Nothin' says lovin' like
a fresh pie from the oven

Love & Scandal
are the best sweeteners of tea

— Henry Fielding

HOME is where the cookies are.

I'm a good egg - just a little cracked.

Calling Children
Strong and able
Clear your dishes
Off the table.

Mothers add
lovin spoonfuls.

Our Budget -
a mathematical confirmation
of our suspicions

A budget:
going broke methodically.

Life's Like That

The Present is a gift

To get out of a hard situation
try a soft answer.

Fate just keeps on happening

In spite of the cost of living, it's still popular.

Humour can make a serious difference

Tell the truth -
There's less to remember.

Facts are stubborn things.

Practice makes perfect
Just be careful what you practice

To improve your outlook
keep looking up

Birthdays are a gift from God
That's why we can't return them

There are two way$ to be rich......
make more or de$ire le$$.

If your mind goes blank...
don't forget to turn off the sound

Life is nothing
like the brochure.

I want to share my ♥ with you.

Homespun with ♥ Love

Love is the source that's strength
Love is the source of life.

Love Begins at Home

When we love ....
we grow.

Two-lips just for you.

A hug a day keeps the grumpies away.

Joined in heart
may the two of us never part

We all grow better with love.

Have you had your hug today?

♥'s that share
♥'s that care

The secret of love is....
to open your ♥

Happiness is being married to your best friend

Our customers are worth a mint to us

shop like a bull.
Charge everything.

Firefighters Save ♥ & Homes

Hair Stylists Are a Cut Above the Rest

Give bus drivers a brake
they know the right of way

Hair stylists are shear pleasure

Hygienists brighten your day.

Pharmacists Rx-tra special.

♥ Nursing is a ♥♥
• work of heart ♥

Give Your Heart to a Nurse

Secretaries are a special type.

Calling in ugly
isn't an acceptable reason
for missing work

No one is unemployed
who minds their own business

I'm not 40 —
I'm 18 with some
extra years of
experience.

Goodbye tension
Hello pension.

Over the hill

Recycled Teenager

Pushing 50...
is exercise enough

We're retired .....
Our job is having a good time.

Aged To Pefection

Forget the hot flashes
Give me some power surges!

"40" Happens.

I'm much too young to look old

You know you're over the hill
when "happy hour"
means "nap time.

Old enough to know better....
Too old to care.

Too old to work
Too young to die
So off into the sunset
Just me & my

We are always the same age inside.
— Gertrude Stein

Aging is when you're a plum
and end up a prune (or need one)

It's never too late
to have a happy childhood

It's hard to be nostalgic...
when you can't remember anything

Me 40!
I demand a recount

Friendship buttons us together.

Mom's Scissors
Hands Off!

Life's a Stitch!

All things are mended
stitch by stitch.

Sew kindness
Gather love.

A gift made by hand is a gift
from the heart

Love is the thread of life

What's Stitched With Love
Will Never Tear

Sewers leave you in stitches!

Don't put all your spools in one basket

Quilter's view a world pieced

On the 8th day God created quilts.

Quilters never come apart at the seams.

A Quilt is...
a Labour of Love

Friends are stitched

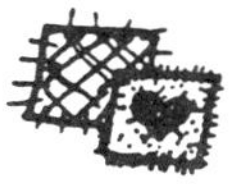

together

by patches of memories

You can always tell a quilter by the thread she wears.

Quilts are patches of love

Days stitched with LOVE rarely unravel.

Happines is...
patching life's pieces together

You can't scare me I teach.

The art of teaching is the art of assisting in discovery

To teach is to learn twice.

— Joubert

If you want children to excel
let them hear all the nice things you say
about them to others

Teachers rule!

Teachers make the Grade.
A+

Books are food for the brain.

Teachers make little ones count.
12354

I don't raise 'em....
I just teach 'em.

A teachers memories can never be erased.

Every adult needs a child to teach
It's the way adults learn

Teachers can't live on apples alone.

You are Beary Special.

Fur coats leave me cold.

Never fear
Teddy bears are near.

Be beary quiet
Baby sleeping.

Bear-ware
Teddies everywhere.

My bear may be ripped & torn
from frolicking about.
but I know my bear still loves me
cuz a bears love cant fall out

Bear bottoms
Welcome Here.

Have you hugged your teddy today?

Don't leave this place unbearable.

Have a Beary Merry Christmas

Everything in life I share
Except of course my teddy bear

Aa Bb Cc Dd Ee Ff Gg
Hh Ii Jj Kk Ll Mm Nn Oo
Pp Qq Rr Ss Tt Uu Vv
Ww Xx Yy Zz & 1 2 3 4
5 6 7 8 9 0

Aa Bb Cc Dd Ee
Ff Gg Hh Ii Jj Kk
Ll Mm Nn Oo Pp
Qq Rr Ss Tt Uu
Vv Ww Xx Yy Zz
& 1 2 3 4 5 6
7 8 9 0

Aa Bb Cc Dd Ee Ff

Gg Hh Ii Jj Kk Ll

Mm Nn Oo Pp Qq

Rr Ss Tt Uu Vv

Ww Xx Yy Zz &

1 2 3 4 5 6 7 8 9 0

Aa Bb Cc Dd Ee Ff Gg

Hh Jj Kk Ll Mm Nn Oo

Pp Qq Rr Ss Tt Uu Vv

Ww Xx Yy Zz &

1 2 3 4 5 6 7 8 9 0

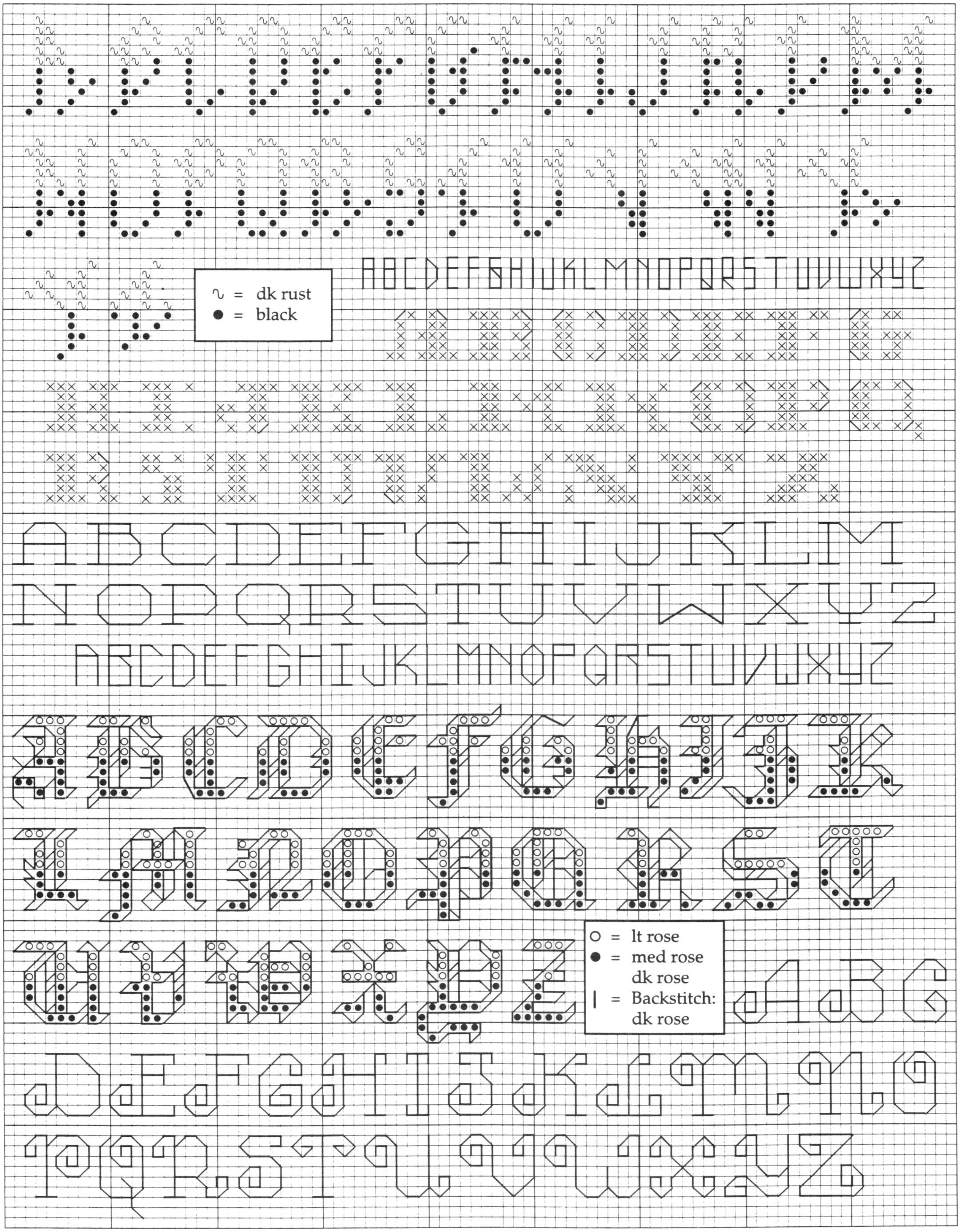

Alphabets reprinted from "The Ultimate Cross Stitch Alphabet Book", with permission of the publisher, American School of Needlework® Inc., ©1992, Kooler Design Studio Inc.

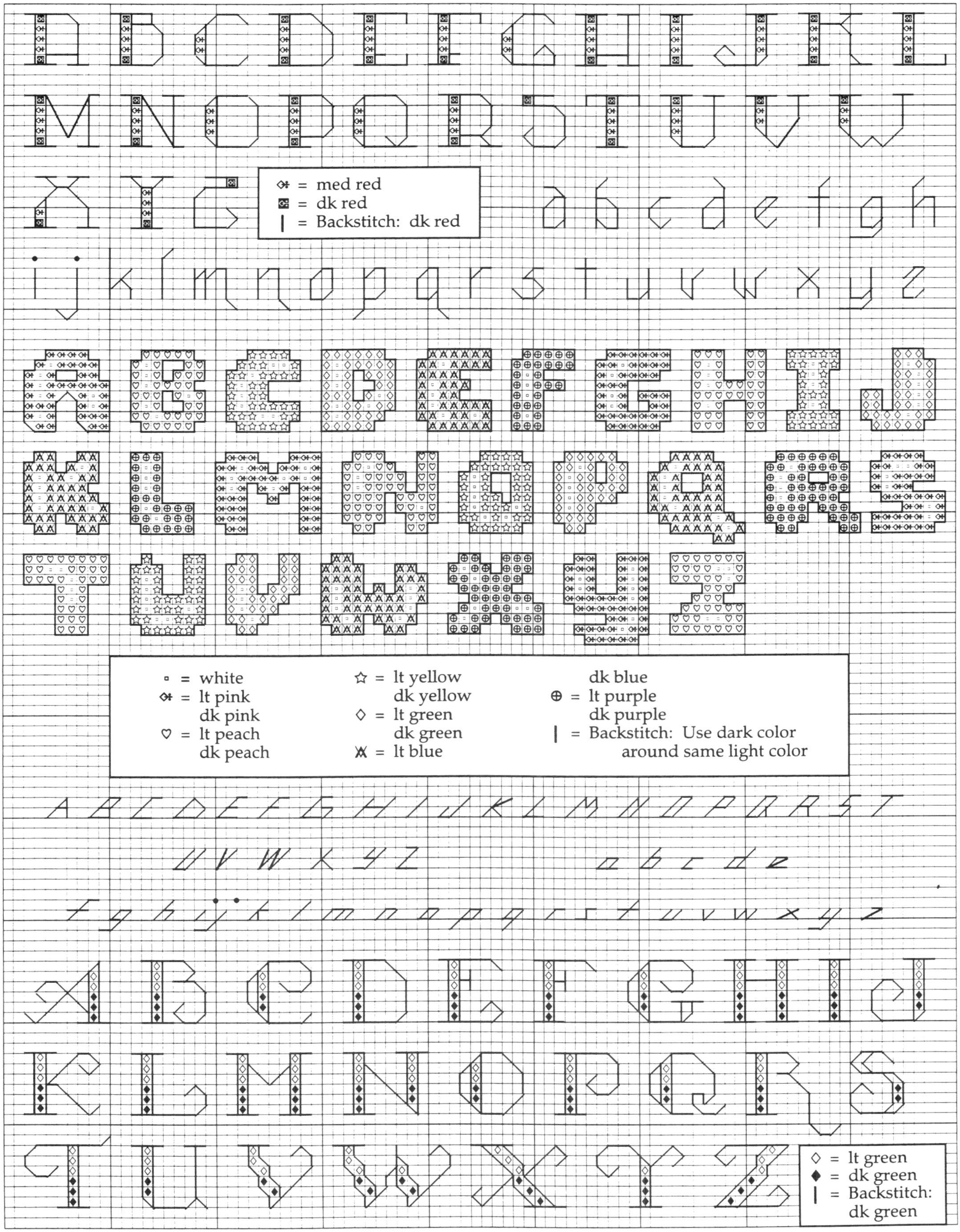

Alphabets reprinted from "The Ultimate Cross Stitch Alphabet Book", with permission of the publisher, American School of Needlework® Inc., ©1992, Kooler Design Studio Inc.